Verse Related

K.S. Davies

Young Welsh and Poetic

2005

Acknowledgements

I would never have had the confidence to write this book without the unerring support of my partner George Moore. Numerous thanks are due to him for reading each poem, for listening, criticising and commending me.

People who encouraged me along the way from my first poem written aged eight include the teachers of Mayals Primary School (1987-1991), Penlan Poets leader Kathleen McVeigh (1989-1991), Bumbles of Mumbles creator Alex Frith (1991) and poet Hilary Llewellyn Williams (1999).

My family have steadfastly believed in my talent and I think it is at last safe to let them read a whole book written by me! I do hope it is worth the wait. Thank you for your patience.

I would like to welcome all new readers to this book and thank you for your support. My website **www.youngwelshandpoetic.com** includes the latest samples of my work, a personalised poetry service and a chance for other young poets to be published. Visit soon and you could be part of a new Welsh wave of talent.

Keep reading,

K.S. Davies

Contents

Ambition

Ambition the right to want to be,
The justification of me.
The rope I grasp
With hopeful hands,
The ledge I find, surefooted.

The cliff that bears
My weighted dreams,
The surge of air
My lungs receive.
The reason I decide to climb,
Revive that critical word.

Carved and set
In Swansea stone,
Twin-towned at my toes.
I step hard on ambition,
Accelerate my goal
Wishing on those Welsh
Born stars who went before
And did not fail.

I want to be the next
In line, glittering
With intent to rise.
Talent seizing spot-light shine,
Drumming up rhythm,
Resonating words
Making that verse related sound,
Poetry, for now.

Paper Heart

I gave you my paper heart
And the verse my nerves
Declared was true.

Chaining myself to your
Image, ensuring that I would
Never forget the way you looked.

My crush, like homemade
Perfume cloyed, petting
Your ego, waiting, wanting

To see you read my
Scrawled guess who,
A coward's claim to love.

I held you once
At the top of the wheel,
Raising your hand with mine, a flag

To wave us down to earth, I wished
We could stay in the sky like birds
Of faith who always mate for life.

Love Song

As we lie
In the swan neck
Of spent love,
My hands play the ivory
Rush of your skin,
Summer smooth
Petal keys
Rhyme in the first chord.

I wear you,
My sash,
The tag of my
Loved by you state.
I am proud,
Rough-touched
By your tree bark
Hands, climbing my sides
Like the too many times
Washed cloth of my shirt.

You prickle like
Raised nerves, rash
And impetuous.
The wire woollen
Fence of your thighs
Curves into my shape
Like the wing
Of our still whirring flight.
As we count down, curl up
And sleep.

Ballgown

The dress smells of him,　　　Long leg, nylon bound.
His dark hair stubbling　　　Tearing the fabric
The sleeve,　　　　　　　　She widens her eyes,
Fingers missing the clasp　　Delighting in his dismay.
Still sliding　　　　　　　　Knowing his ears hear every
Beneath the V cut velvet,　　Ripping step she makes.
Her skin a spear.　　　　　　Her ladder of escape.

She looks as he wants
Her to look,
Grown up, dressed up,
Shoes inscribing her
Pain on the scrubbed tiles.

The clink of her long
Chained pearls is a
Clashing of teeth.
She squirms
In her designer chrysalis,
Waiting for wings,
Fighting the harsh
Precision of hair grips.

Her curls are too
Well coiled and secured,
Nails too false too
Sealed with polish,
Drumming her thigh
Like sharpened shells,
Watching, catching him
Staring.
Deliberately she unwinds,
Bends from the waist
With aerobic grace,
Trailing the knife edged
Nail of her thumb
Down the line of her

Dissecting The Row

Dark of spirit
He snatches my line,
Jeering, he deepens
It, steering it low
With his bass throated
Accent, a tongue twisting
Snake, stealing my sentiment,
Turning it

Into something more
Than I ever meant,
He adds some spite,
Some lies, some gain
And digging it up
With his hurt pride trowel
He stands there
Earth and words.

I wonder if I
Should touch him
But he's animal mad
And trembling,
Taking the next jibe
In to digest with the retch
Drawing mix of 'leave me'
lines

Why did I say it?
I meant it then,
Meant to be free
Of his tortured eyes,
His hands caught out
Of his pockets fidgeting,
Scratching his rage
On the worn belt buckle,
Holding my plea, refusing it.

I thought I could
Be alone and lose
The feather down
Comfort of his very
Presence by folding myself
To a cross armed
Knee to chin shape.
But he found me,
Unfurled me
And pressed me to him
And I'm still in that moment,
Waking.

Now as he asks me
To relive the fight
I close off the edge
To his voice and hide
In the thought that
He loves me
And I love him.
Through every attempt
To assault my heart
It beats still for him
And our day to day life,
Sparring.

The Best Of...

We were friends,
True friends, so
Everyone said,
I trusted, invested
My time in her,
Lending my ear,
My shoulder, my soul.
Letting her see me,
The real me,
My thoughts,
Confusing as they were
Could not match hers
For fantastical flights
Of more than fancy.

It was as if
Her great bright
Cauldron of
Simmering daydreams
Spilled.

Scorching and drenching me,
Her belief blazed
On in me.
Raising me high
On the crest
Of a dragon's breath
Flaming and breaking
To slivers of light,
Trailing, remaining
As floating smoke circles.
I started to think
In this dizzying place,
On a high,
On a flight
To a bigger beyond.
Using her

As a template
For me, my life.

I lost her
Spinning through dreams
That were not
My own
I reached and
Found her gone
Long gone.
Higher again but
Without me now,
Not wishing to share
Or take my hand,
I watched her twirl,
A silent dance,
A flourish of fingers
Proud, unlinked.
I caught the bow
Of her back
Turned on me
Signifying the end.

Relationships

The Grandchild's Garden

The garden was Manderley to me,
Wild and tiny paths entwined in
Lovers knots and blossom, fronds
Of mint green leaves apologetic,
Bowing with unexplained fruit,
The wings of ladybirds an added
Splash, a red and black dice thrown,
Sent winging, wishing.
Her burden a secret.

My wish was to grow still smaller,
Doll short, fairy crowned familiar
With the curled fists of flowers,
Gnarled acorn caps, dew to fill
Thimbles and soil to mould
My perfect face with eyes of seed
And grassy hair, the budding rose
Dust mouth, no thorns for the children,

Only the heavenly haze of honey-suckle
Stinging my senses, the swing,
Its song note low like the piano stool
At home, grasshopper still in the moment
Before his vibrato cry.
I felt myself shrink to belong.

Your Cross

You embroidered the cross
At Easter, an offering
Not for church
But for ourselves,
Reminding us
Of the season's holy story,
The sacrifice and rise to life.

Your cross was celtic crafted
With intricate stitching,
Multi-threads, magenta,
Jade, cerise
And ruby red
For blood and shame,
Taken in our place.

It made more sense to me
To see it body abandoned,
Left with the imprint of his
Gift and there in those
Tumultuous strands
I saw him,
More than a ghost.

Hay-On-Wye (The First)

Dedicated to George, Valentine's Day 2005

November blazed, defiant
Sun torched, wrapping
Itself around us, our scarf,
Our gloves and winter coat
That held us fast on our first holiday.
Set free on a town of books.

We were readers, explorers,
Lovers fingers locked.
And hand to page we turned
To raise the cover delving in.
At pace we devoured Hay Chocolate
And fireside safe declared our love.
Sip-kissing Capari you told me
You loved like a psychopath
And drawing your stare from
Your eyes into mine.
I believed you, unafraid.

Later illuminated streamers fell,
Threading the streets with stark
Bright bursting sound. We ran,
Craving the warmth of our rented room,
The flower strewn spread, the books
Piled high on each side
And each other, we met in the middle
And lay there looking, eye searching,
Smile greeting still.

To Youth

Youth disillusioned grows
From grace, from innocence
To wasted bloom,
To be picked and discarded.

Eyes wilted, defensive
Stare, lost in the
Concrete grey of pavements,
And black hood caves,

Alcoholic orange fizzes,
Spirit strong and cider spiked
Youth begins to shed the skin
Of baby soft beginnings.

Clothes are used as
Courtship capes, a mini seductress
Struts and stalks her way
To a tearful cab ride home.

Snub nose firmly stuck in books
She travels and borrows backpack lives.
A year for the road and a gift wrapped
Slice of world is taken home.

The end is always near as
Youth stops calling, overtakes
And shouts 'I'm leaving now, not coming back.'
She watches, growing old.

Mountain Beer

His first sip is cool,
A trickling touch
Slips down his throat,
An ice bitter river
Topped with mountain snow.

He remembers his father
Calling through wet wool,
The top note lost
In the wind whipped sleet
And the long skid down
On damaged soles.

His boots now abandoned,
A sodden tangle
Of laces, mud
Encrusted leather,
Cracked and panting,
Tongues curled in
From the taste of dirt.

This pint is restoring
His faith in drink
The yellow gem glow of
Its body fire-lit.
The last few bubbles
Of froth dispersing.

Outside the white sky flickers
Spins out,
A sprinkling of snowflakes,
That settle like dust
On the hood of his father's coat
Zipped down with the slow
buzz
Of bar chat,
The sing-song tingle

Of loose coins.

Glass in hand
He toasts the day.
The sheep on the hill,
His son running
On but beside him now,
The beer bringing warmth
To his belly
With the ease of melting snow.

His Mother

Meeting her I search
For him, take the hand
That held his tears,
See the smile that
Warmed him grow
Uneasy and release me.
Palm from palm
She stands up straighter.
Vixen eyes appraising,
Chasing the signs of
Why I am right for him.

Her hair, side parted
And severe tops the robust
busying form of
Her jumper and jeans front.
She is anxious to
Appear calm, tea-making
Cake-baking, calm and
Composed, a china cup
Hostess saved for best.

As a cook she is
Comforting, offering
Plates of mash, meat
And cauliflower, cheese
Topped toast, there is
Something for all and
The table is full with welcome
And chat and jostling elbows
Fighting for knife and fork
freedom.
I'm safe when I find him
The turn of her head
Reminds me of his day,
The way he tells me,
I soften at her side, listen,

Compare and there is his
Voice as he breaks in,
Across, I'm seeing his
Childhood and understanding
All he has lost.

The Crowd

Those people, not real
I don't call friends.
Where are they now?
Do they wait in corners?
The decadent smile of
Their blunt dagger charms
A harmless snare.

Do they pounce?
And pretend to be alive
Behind their absinthe green
Glazed eyes, they hide it well,
With a nicotine puff and wallet
Drawn silver, heavy with change.

Once the whirl of the drink
Contained them, bringing their
Waltzer nights out to a lurch
And thudding stop.
But now they embrace
The turn of a world
That raises them to the stage.

They relish performance, the
Sound of their voices enriched
By the burgundy brown bitter pint,
Chasers to sweeten and cheers
To demand that the last man
Standing pay his round.
The toasts made under the table.

Snow Petals

Snow petals fall
At the wedding,
In a flurry of sugar
Spun rain.
Soft flakes catch
In the web of the
Veil, masking the face
Of the weather shy bride.

The groom is impatient
And brushes the waves
Of slow falling paper
Away from his eyes.
He is already on honeymoon
Time, he sees nothing but paradise.

But when he lies down
Beside his new wife,
He'll remember the torrent
Of wishes he scorned,
The snow of white weddings,
The lighthearted blessings,
Crushed at the open church door.

To Iris

Named for a flower
You grew long-stemmed
And blushing, blossomed,
Leaving your down
To earth sense, well buried,
In the border where
We made mud pies.

You stole blue shadow
Trailing its pastel crumbs
In the sink, on the floor
As you fled, skirts flowing,
Full, hand sewn where the hem
Slipped Iris, deep and
Caught your heel.

You skipped back then
And your dark curls fell,
Breaking the rhythmic
Plaiting of each day's
Sensible hair-do.
Defying the comb and
The deft mother's hand
That shaped us all.

I admired you, as art,
A painting I could
Have crafted myself
With the wild hands
Of wanting to be grown up
And follow you, through
Clipped dance steps and
Stilted small talk, into
The tidy compact world,
Just outside the door.

Snow Bed

My bed enfolds me
In quilted snow,
The sheets are like
Thin ice moulding
My skin, with polished
Caresses from silver-lined palms.

And as I dissolve
In my liquid thoughts,
I float in the heart
Of a winter scene,
Sketching my frosted
Breath over the night.
Behind my eyes my sight is cold.

By morning my pillows
Are marked with deep hollows,
The footprints of dream makers,
I'm left behind.
Magic lives on in the sleeping stars,
Hiding their light
As I wake and thaw.

Seaweed

Seaweed holds out
Dead fingers,
Clutching at the land.
Claiming it with slimy folds
And wreath-like, dripping
Mermaid's hair,
Pungent with salt
And shell-worn shoals,
Swarming with cold fleshy creatures
That crawl on the stones
Of the dried out land.

Glimmering wet, the coils of green
Unfurl like smoke from a witch's broom.
Emerald flesh on fragile bones,
Decaying scent of death.
The mourners are seagulls,
Their pitiful screams vie with the wail
Of the banshee sea.
Swooping with empty shame
They sting the sand with acid tears,
Burying the sea-torn hands
That cannot wave goodbye.

Song of a Mermaid

As waves play on
The braille rainbow of her scales,
They see in her
A world of colours.
Shades of a love
That shells still hold
In echoes and whispers
Beneath the tide.

And her words fall singing
Filled with the rich notes
Of her heart,
Sighing – high on the salt sprayed
Rocks, crying on cliff-tops
Joined by the wild and turning
Wings, in a chorus of gulls,
Who have no pride.

She dives and her hair
Is heavy with sea,
Gleaming in all its jewelled light.
She returns to the womb,
The water that bears her.

In circles of sorrow.
She knows that the sky
Is just a reflection,
Of passing clouds.
But in her song she flies.

Cat Quest

A narrowed
Cat glance
And a wistful stare,
Follows her tail
Tipped white
To farewell.

Fur glistens
Like dew-grass,
Painted black.
And deep in the
Animal canvas
Shines his crest.

He has passed
Through green
Grazed pathways,
Clawed through
The dawn light
Under cloud.

And now
His sodden paws
Seek retreat.
There is rain in his eyes
And he lingers
Looks on, into the house,
Through the closed door,
Sensing her purr.

Field Vole

A vole is a child's animal,
Hide and seeking, hopscotch dodging.
Pointing ballerina toes
His pink shell claws crab-borrowed.

Sniffing bulb and bark detecting
He is plant attuned and sensing
Life breath in their roots unearths
The deep wedged anchor of his food store.

Mattress moist, his tussock waits,
His low vole furry pod of self
Substantial, small, defending his space.
With all his high ferocious words,
A babbling battle chant grows.

A kestrel spies his glow worm
Scented trail, he swoops, his
Spark off running with the green
Reed stems, runaway strong like
A brown grass blade or a child
Of the field, at play.

Mare

Grey, not white the mare,
Her bride's veil mane like
Frothing lace against her
Long neck, ladylike, serene

She stands and curls a hoof
Her eyes dance flashing, the
Lashes pearl clear, nose in
The air she backs to distance

Herself from the man at her
Side, the man who whispers
The fields to life and rides
To belonging for them both.

He dwells but does not farm,
The yellow rapeseed butters the
View for two to devour but she
Hides her eyes, she is pure.

A Greyhound Retires

He should race in that coat
Under moleskin, sleek tight
Fur, he should race and win
With his bone sharp thighs
The lean greed strains
For the field, the game,
To be in the lead, not on it,
Not living the
Puppet poor life of a pet.

He should take on the
Next dog head to head
And dart eared press
His advantage, the burn
Of his paws in the dust
And the storm of confusion,
The fog and the pulse of
His first past the post
Surge and breath

Sent panting, he gasps
Like an old man
Once in training, laying
His head down low
Where the hand strokes
His nose and feeds him,
Admiring his delicate skull
Cap face and the frail body
That used to fly.

Tracing the Leaf

Skeletal fragments
Fine-boned, haunted.
Run with the silver
Lick of veins,
The thread of glitter,
Green and gold.

Light splits to a rainbow
But unites colour
Shining through bright stripes,
A curved spectrum.

While the sky is keening,
Wild hot breath
On a winter face.
The leaf plains are quivering,
Strength in the drain
Of sapless waste.

Icicles frost the shaking hand,
Shedding its colour,
The mist, skin to dust.
In the crispness of change
It grows cracked with the wind
And torn as parchment, ages.

Winter Storm

Angel cold the wet
Nosed rain became
A crochet shower,
Star-shaped, bon-bon
Powdery, tentative,
Childlike, shy and soft.

Heightening my sense
Of self, my body shocked,
Touched as though bare
Was chilled and warned
And stirred by puffed up
White bird cloud.

Ready to shake its
Moulted tail feather
Down, in my belted
Suede I raced the
Snow, as though I too
Could drift and skip

As a flying speck
Of winter life set
Soaring, poured
From a frozen sky
To the brave defiance of
My cheek, a melting
Windblown kiss.

Clementine

Citrus front peeled back
Exposes flakes of pithy snow.
River divided islands,
Waste deserted, lonely ground.

Ripped from the rounded shoulders
Of a luscious juicy queen.
Her cape laid down, a cast off home
Becomes an open palm.

A map drawn bare from trickling lines
Depicts her death bed scene
As she rolls forth her orange flesh
Frees sacrificial sweetness.

Skin undone, her body swells,
Breaks to a new segmented self,
A ring of half-moon faces flattered
To be hungered for.

Eden

I walk through marble halls,
Back to the pure, thought-filled
Land, the first world where
Nature is clean and spare,
Crafted by hands that inspire no faith,
Hands that no longer hold our pain.

I walk through the archway
Of knitted grass, dew
Falls like tears
From the eyes of a child.
Daisies are chained
In a crystal ball.
Our future is broken
To shattered glass.

Snake-like the darkness falls
And turns in the grip of a poisonous snare.
Bold voices drown the whisper of peace
And claim its beating heart.
I breath the last of the sinless air,
Already mist has laced the sky
With dainty flecks of innocent life,
Feathers of rising fear.

The Death Of Autumn

Fragile branches, broken bark
Peels away the strips
Of summer.

Leaves cling on, in aged splendour,
Ripe bright colours
Worn as armour.

They will fight, against their fate,
Crumpled defiant
They line the ground.

Crackling beneath the feet of children,
Tired fireworks,
Losing heart.

Frost may weave its delicate strands
Over the earth
The trees, the leaves.

Under the white cold autumn dies,
Huddled in corners
Stirred by the breeze.

Each breath leaves more slowly,
Softer than snow
As it falls in earthly silence.

White Night

It could have been dew
Or else your ghost,
A clammy white sky spirit
Sent to drip

An ethereal trail,
Tick-stopped hands
Of a dandelion clock
Unwound

On the back of a grass
Land drinking stars
'Til the thirst is purged
And the day calls dry and hoarse.

Sun Goddess

Her hands are warm
Like the wings
Of fireflies.
She sees colours
Through golden eyes.
She takes the rain
As her life-force
Stealing tears
From flowers
To quench her thirst.

She is a liquid queen
With lips like delicate
Candle flames.
Her yawns devour sky
And sting the clouds
Until they serpent hiss,
Brush against her hair
And catch alight like waxen dolls
Gleaming, polished statues,
Distorted by her breath.

Dusk descends
And runs her silky fingers
Through the curls of cloud.
The goddess lines her cloak
With darker colours
As she smiles down.
Winking like topaz,
Rich and refined,
Clothed in the grace
Of a thousand stars,
Slowly she bows
And hides her face
In a mirror of moon lit night.

Opening The Story Door

The door to a story is never closed
But always just ajar.
It offers an enchanting glimpse
Of a world beyond our lives,
Shining, inviting, a spiralling tale
Of romance, trust and greed.

Brimming with words
That tumble from page to page,
Speaking beneath the cover
In earthy tones, alive and overgrown
With glorious expression.
From muted sighs and whispers,
To booming speech to verse,
And roaring raucous laughter
In moments of mirth.

Characters become our friends
As we breath in their spirited selves,
Move and progress with their story
Wrapped up in layers of plot,
We turn towards a conclusion
And wish that we could dwell
In the magic of words forever,
Drifting, with the tide of their song.

The Winning Team

So the red jersey wins,
The dragon flies.
The Triple Crown, the Grandslam
Won by team feet kicking
Up wonder turf,
And precious hands to hoist
The people's dream, belief
Held high, the trophy team,
The Celtic side will grace the
Home grown history page.
The new Welsh child will read
Of the silver booted strike,
The Shane style shimmy,
The glory trail from England
Back to Wales, the final game
Of giant strength and green
Defending, grim faced scrums.
And at the end the one team
Stands kaleidoscope strong,
Collecting colours, shirts and hearts,
Through power play, impassioned
Truth in tries and rucks, the old
Welsh school emerges scarlet
Branded land of our fathers,
The land of winners today.

The Song

I hear the song I knew before,
Before I was wise, before I knew me.
All I knew then was the sound,
The song, the pure melody
Of meandering streams
The warm sentiment
Of a voice that is known.

Now I am older and further away,
Alone in my rules that I set for myself
And still the song calls me
Draws me from myself, into
Its movement, the small
Contained space, which holds its spell.

The song is a flower
Pressed flat, drained of perfume,
Marking the dust of a folded page,
Tuned in the key of a precious time
The rippling sound cascades and slides
Leaving one last triumphant note,
Remembered, held and saved.

Apprentice Angel

These wings are yours
If you can hold a whisper,
Take a violin string, stop
Its sigh and blend each note
To melancholic triumph.

If you wear music,
Skin to inside, warm
With melodious fire, your
Voice a silk-worm's fluid
Reams with strength
To pull an audience in.

You'll fit, you'll do,
Ornament enough for
Pride of place upon my
Mantelpiece, a magic emblem
Otherwordly, white unsettled,
Stage poised.

I will build your halo
With a ribbon winding
Gold on wire and tinsel,
Christmas past proclaiming,
Standing as the me I hide.
Your knowing china eyes.

Engaged

Ruby multi-faceted love
When placed on gold
Flame throws,
The crimson light
Of tomorrow
Day's demise,
A fine forecast.

The bashful flush
Of boy and girl,
Precarious steps along the pier,
Made safe from hand to hand,
The sea majestic masses.

The scent of salt
Is clean and showers
Strong upon the lovers
Faces, turning to each other
And the rose blood flicker
Of the stone.

Factory Base

The slatterns at work belch
Blue fire from the gut
And heart wrench, mourning cleaner lives,
Breathing their woes to the sky.

The stacks, school-marm
Severe are lofty, piping psalms
To grown up children, listening no longer,
Squatting small, cylindrical.

Steam, entranced entrails
Take form as white and shocking
Manes, ghostly scudding cloud-like,
Clawing, shade for factory base

Outpouring, pure emotion moves
To force the industry into removing,
Its black block mask, the struggle
Revealed to on go and upturn.

Doll

Serenity smiles upon her face,
Quietly, unobtrusively near,
Brushing her features with gentle strokes,
Lending an unspoken dignity.
Cherubic and clear her cheeks of the rose
Blush softly and faintly like summer night sky.
Perfectly formed coils of corn-blessed hair
Are locked up in ribbons and carefully tied.

Prettily absent her crystal eyes stare
As if they might take in the world
Or all time.
As if they might break through the glass that
Contains them, scattering bright blue, long lashed charm.
Her hands, folded neatly are cold, white and still,
Held in one moment that lingers.

What does she see behind her screen?
Within her demure sights, does life begin?
She had been moulded in stone-like thought,
Caught in a day-dream where beauty is all
And illusion has no need to speak or feel,
Only to stare with sightless eyes,
Winking like stars behind cloud.

Kitchen Canvas

Red blooded fruit
Oozing its flesh,
Weeping its knife-
Sliced head in my hands.
Raining, its speckled seed
Gleaming, encased.
Eyes ripe

Watching inelegant
Steel silhouetted, looming
The menacing lift of
The lid, heralds the quagmire.
The slow drip,
Of sauce.

The diamond sketched floor
Is a kitchen canvas
Spreading the stains like
Blotting paper. Drawing them
Into misshapen mirth.
Like the corners of
Your mouth.

If only it swallowed,
Sucked on the tail end
Of my laziness. Tongue like
A sponge head, lapping at
Leftovers, soaking up scraps.

A polythene nest to a brood
Of crumbs, rustles rebellious,
Taunting the bin, as if it might
Fill it to tiptop
Brimful bliss.

But the tiles are languid,
Wallowing in the new
Found mud of my craft.
Cans disinclined to right
Themselves or stop
The rude brute slap of their
spills.

They want to paint
And my hand, free fumbling
For cupboard space, tumbles
The flour, releasing its
Mist like a cloud driven mad.
Coating the scene with shame.

The Wounded Boat

He kneels in the twilight
Spinning moon disc hot
With the surgical grind
Of steel, the bleed now sparking
Scarlet sick and weeping
Fire from the fountain wound.

The trawler sprawls,
Unburdened body still,
Save lapping water,
Veins, numb heart confined,

As the silhouette witness
Sweeps the bridge with
Her overcoat train,
An overhead shadow
Shameful crows,
Stealing the vessel's life.

Off The Rails

At midnight the town
Travels, swallowed as snake
Joined dot to dot
Houses, breathing through
Windows, illusion borne
Currents, electric gold,
Mirrored and flaming.

In my mind I control
It, a plastic snake
Snapping, each click
Of each segment
A jut of its hipless
Wavering song.

Holding the train
Between thumb
And forefinger,
I throw the trails
From each mapped out
Journey, lacing the paths
Of luminous strangers,
Chained like fairy lit pearls.

The span of my hand,
A flesh webbed cloud,
Covers their eyes and
Becomes their earth.
Until I let go and they
Hurtle, back on the rails
Into time tabled stops
And changes.

Boat Blue

River shell you're beached and dry,
Hollow within your painted hide.
And yet, your colours swell and call
Pooling in loss, without sand.

Bright as cloud scared
Sky, and blue in the young boy's eyes.
You remind him of summer,
Before it hits the tide.

You are the joyful diversion
That he dreams, free from harm.
But in years when he wakes you will
Carry him, into the waiting waves

Made Up

Opening her eyes with kohl
She finds a deeper green.
She watches, defines the oval
Smudging the line beneath.

Powdery shadow daubs her
With uneven shine, gathering
Drawing the crease of her eye,
Down with the slope of her lazy gaze.

Up, the indignant wand
Mascaras, each lash clings to
The other. An inky, linking
Chain, black with spider kisses.

Cosmetic shame blushes from her cheeks like
Waxen fruit, heavy lips drip gloss
And her painted smile blooms full,
Brimful with scented promise.

I Declare Time

I declare time,
I call the alarm.
I watch as you rise
And I sense breath and form.
My eyes in the clock face
My hand on each hour,
My heart in each second
Ticks steadily.
I'm held behind glass,
But I'm singing the change.
I'm driving the slow-step,
The quick-step, the flight.

I'm read but I don't read,
I merely perform,
Wound in
A circle that I walk alone.
Others spin round me
And think they might pass,
But I am ahead
And my time moves on.
I don't claim to own it,
Just to be close,
Just to be windblown by its force.
Feeling it running
Through my wooden veins,
Like filtered sand.

The Dinosaur In My Coffee Cup

Deep in the mocha cavern stirred the dinosaur.
The steam drew me closer, so hunched up was I,
The coffee cup ceased to reflect me
And in my place rose he.

Meeting his eyes, bold from the crystal mud I saw
The drip of his mirthful jaws and knew their dilated truth.
Rough was the tilt of his head
And laurel wreathed with shell,
Jagged plated armour
The steel in each shuddering step.

Inhaling the sweet muddled smell of syrup
Tarred with his thick breath, bitter, spent,
I opened up belief once more,
Relayed to me from pale back-light,
Diffused by glass, to cup, to view.
I knew I would hold the hump of his past
And trace the elongated longing of his neck,
Back to my daydream, bubble formed colourful muse.

And who would have thought the skeletons we see
Loftily framing and haunting the dust of museums
Would be reborn of flesh and given teeth?
Enough to lend sneer to his liquid channelled roar.
Alive in a parallel coffee cup, cooling in my hand.

Death

Death, a silver bellied eel
Will writhe and squirm
And wormlike fish its
Stone mad eyes from the
Depths of its hollow insides,
Out-turn the curious
Pink flesh that shows
It was once alive, to be
Preyed upon and spat upon
And told it was far too legless
To be proud,
To be anything but
A slime ridden sea water
Animal, evading the hook.